MACHINE LEARNING FOR BEGINNERS

Jonathan S. Walker

Copyright © 2017 Jonathan S. Walker
All rights reserved.

DEDICATION

This Book Is Dedicated To All Who Desire To Be Financially Free. May Your Efforts Bear Fruits In the Near Future And I Wish You All The Success In Life.

&

I dedicate this book as well to my two beautiful children and my loving wife who have been nothing short of being my light and joy throughout the years.

Copyright 2017 by Jonathan S. Walker - All rights reserved.

The following eBook is reproduced below with the goal of providing information that is as accurate and reliable as possible. Regardless, purchasing this eBook can be seen as consent to the fact that both the publisher and the author of this book are in no way experts on the topics discussed within and that any recommendations or suggestions that are made herein are for entertainment purposes only. Professionals should be consulted as needed prior to undertaking any of the action endorsed herein.

This declaration is deemed fair and valid by both the American Bar Association and the Committee of Publishers Association and is legally binding throughout the United States.

Furthermore, the transmission, duplication or reproduction of any of the following work including specific information will be considered an illegal act irrespective of if it is done electronically or in print. This extends to creating a secondary or tertiary copy of the work or a recorded copy and is only allowed with express written consent from the Publisher. All additional right reserved.

The information in the following pages is broadly considered to be a truthful and accurate account of facts and as such any inattention, use or misuse of the information in question by the reader will render any resulting actions solely under their purview. There are no scenarios in which the publisher or the original author of this work can be in any fashion deemed liable for any hardship or damages that may befall them after undertaking information described herein.

Additionally, the information in the following pages is intended only for informational purposes and should thus be thought of as universal. As befitting its nature, it is presented without assurance regarding its prolonged validity or interim quality. Trademarks that are mentioned are done without written consent and can in no way be considered an endorsement from the trademark holder.

CONTENTS

Part 1

Introduction
Chapter One: Machine Learning
Chapter Two: Big Data
Chapter Three: Reversion with Machine Learning
Chapter Four: Python and Machine Learning
Chapter Five: Neural Networks and Deep Learning
Chapter Six: Installing Free Datasets for Machine Learning

PART 2

Chapter One: Data Analytic Basics
Chapter Two: Challenges for Data Analytics
Chapter Three: Terms You Need to Know for Data Analysis
Chapter Four: Benefits of Data Analysis
Chapter Five: The Risks Involved with Data Analysis
Chapter Six: Types of Data Analysis
Conclusion

VIP Subscriber List

Dear Reader, If you would like to receive latest tips and tricks on internet marketing, exclusive strategies, upcoming books & promotions, and more, do subscribe to my mailing list in the link below! I will be giving away a free book that you can download right away as well after you subscribe to show my appreciation!

Here's the link: http://bit.do/jonathanswalker

Introduction

With Machine learning, you are going to have the ability to solve more complex issues with python. With all of the technology that you have at your disposal, you are going to be inputting data into your program and getting an outcome.

When you can understand how machines learn and work, you are going to better understand how to get the results that you are wanting from the program that you are working with. Machines may seem complex, but after you understand them, you are not going to be confused as to why you are not getting the outcome that you wanted in the first place.

You had plenty of other books that you could have used in order to learn about machine learning, but thank you for purchasing this one!

Chapter One: Machine Learning

When you hear the word machine learning, it is going to be referring to the subfield found in PC science where PCs are given the tools needed to learn without being programmed by a person.

The evolution of this study has come to include pattern recognition as well as the learning theory that can be found in the artificial intelligence field. The machines are going to explore the study and learn how to construct algorithms that are going to be learned from and be able to make predictions with the data that is provided for these algorithms like overcoming the static programming instructions. These instructions are going to be driven by data for predictions or decisions to be made by building a model from the simple inputs of data.

Machine learning is typically employed through a range of computing tasks where algorithms are designed and carried out with superior performance. An example of this is the sorting that your email does in an effort to keep your email secure.

Machine learning tends to overlap with PC statistics where predictions are made through a PC that has strong ties to be able to optimize mathematical equations. This also makes it to where theories, methods, and applications dominate the field.

Machine learning is also often confused with data mining which consists of data analysis. This data analysis is also known as unsupervised learning. While machine learning can be unsupervised, it is going to have to learn as well as establish a baseline for its behavior before finding meaningful anomalies.

In the data analytic field, machine learning is going to be used in order to create methods that are complex along with algorithms that are going to be used in predictions. These predictions are known as predictive analytics when used commercially. The predictions are going to enable researchers, analysts, engineers, and data scientists in making reliable decisions as a way to uncover any insights that may be hidden by learning from historical relationships and data trends.

Back in 2016, machine learning was made a buzzword for the Gartner hype circle while it was at the peak of its inflated expectations. Due to the fact that finding patterns is difficult, there is often not enough training to go around.

Problems and tasks

Machine learning is typically classified into three categories depending on the nature of the learning.

1. Unsupervised learning: labels are not going to be given for the learning algorithms that are used which is going to leave it to find its own structure in the input. Unsupervised learning is going to be a goal that you can use in finding patterns that are hidden in the

data that you are using or as a means to an end.
2. Supervised learning: your PC is going to be given inputs as well as the outcome that you are going to want so that the PC can learn a general rule in how to map out the input and outcomes.
3. Reinforcement learning: there is going to be a PC program that works with a dynamic environment to perform specific goals such as when you are playing a game against an opponent. The program will give you feedback in terms of punishments and rewards as it navigates the space of the problem.
4.
5. There is a semi supervised learning that is going to fall between supervised and unsupervised. This is going to be when you are going to give training signals that are not complete with the training set so that the program has to do some of the work.
6.
7. Transduction is going to be whenever the principle takes on the entire problem such

as learning times. But this is not going to work whenever there are targets missing.
8.
9. Machine learning also includes categories such as learning to learn where the program is going to learn the inductive bias of the program based on experiences that have happened before. Developmental learning is going to be the same as robot learning where the program is going to be able to generate its own sequence from the learning situations that it is put through so that it can acquire repertoires of novel skills through self-exploration and interactions with humans and other programs.
10.
11. Yet another category of machine learning is going to happen when you consider what the outcome is from the machine learning system.
12.
1. The classification of inputs is going to be divided into at least two classes where the user is going to have to produce a model that is going to take the inputs that are not

seen by the user from these classes. This is going to usually happen in supervised learning such as when your email filters between spam and not spam.
2. Reversion is also going to be supervised for the outcomes to be continuous instead of being discrete.
3. Clustering is going to take the input sets and divide them into various groups. However, the difference between clustering and classification is that the groups are not going to be known to the user before they are made which makes this an unsupervised task.
4. Density estimation is going to locate the distribution of the inputs in that space.
5. Dimensionality reduction takes the input and simplifies it so they can be mapped to the lowest dimension.
6. Topic modeling will take a problem from the program that is inserted by a user and tasked to see if the documents that were inserted cover related topics.
7.
8. A classification machine learning model is

going to be able to be validated by a technique that uses accuracy estimation such as holdout. Holdout is going to split the data when training and testing your set before evaluating the performance of the model on the test set. However, if you look at n fold cross validation then you are going to see that the data will randomly be split into subsets where the k-1 instances are going to be used in training the model while the k instance is going to be used in testing the predictive ability of the training model that you are using.

9.
10. Along with this, the holdout and the cross-validation method is going to use samples for the n instances where the replacement comes from the data set and how it is going to be able to be used in assessing the model's accuracy.
11.
12. On top of that, there is an overall accuracy that an investigator finds, it is going to be reported for specificity and sensitivity such as the true positive rate and the true

negative rate which means that the true positive rate and the true negative rate are going to sometimes report false positive rates or false negative rates.

13.

14. But, it is these rates that are going to fail to show the numerator and denominator for the equation. Your total operating characteristic is going to be an effective method that is going to show the models diagnostic abilities. Total operating characteristic is also going to reveal the numerators and denominators that were mentioned previously in the rates which will mean that the total operating characteristic is going to show you more information than you were able to use with the receiver operating characteristic which is going to fall under the area under the curve.

15.

16. Due to what it is, machine learning often times brings up a lot of ethical questions. The systems that are trained to work with the data that you collect is going to be biased based on the exhibits that the biases

are going to be used on which is going to digitalize the cultural prejudices. Therefore, the responsibility that comes from collecting data is going to be a big part of machine learning.
17.
18. Due to the language that you use when dealing with machine learning, you are going to be using machines that are trained on bias.

Chapter Two: Big Data

It seemed that 2012 was the year that the big data technologies came around and were everything to everyone. But, in 2013 big data analytics became the thing. When you get ahold of substantial amounts of data, you are going to have to manage it but you are also going to want to pull out the most useful information from the collections, and this is going to be a more difficult challenge. Big data is not only going to change the tools that you use, but it is also going to change the way that people think about the extraction and interpretation of data.

Usually, data science is going to be trial and error which is going to be impossible whenever working with data sets that are larger and heterogeneous. However, the more data that is available, there are usually going to be less options that are going to be constructed for the predictive model's due to the fact that there are not going to be many tools that are going to have the capacity to process a large amount of data in a reasonable amount of time. Also, the traditional statistical solutions are going to focus on the analytics that is static which is going to limit the analysis samples that are frozen in time and are typically going to give you results that are surpassed and unreliable.

25.
26. But, there are other alternatives that are going to fix the problems that you have about research domains that are going to be expanded, and this is going to be machine learning. Statistics and PC science have applications coming out that are going to focus on the development of algorithms that are going to be fast and efficient for processing data in real time with the goal being to deliver predictions that are accurate.

27.
28. There are applications that are going to be used in business cases such as telling them how much product they should buy or to

detect fraud. The techniques used in machine learning also solve application problems like figuring out statistics in real time as well as giving a reliable analysis by using generic and automatic methods in order to simplify the data scientist tasks.

29.
30. Chapter Three: Reversion with Machine Learning
31.
32. When looking at statistical modeling, you will notice that reversion analysis is going to be the process of estimating the various relationships you see between variables. This is going to include the techniques that you use when analyzing and modeling several variables at once whenever you are focused on showing the relationship between an independent and dependent variable.
33.
34. Reversion analysis is going to assist you in understanding how the usual value for the dependent variable is going to change while the independent variable is not going to change. Reversion is also going to estimate the conditional expectation of the variable that is dependent based on the independent variable and the average value of that variable.
35.
36. Less commonly, you are going to see the

quantile or the location parameters for the conditional distribution of the variable that is dependent based on what the independent variable is. In most cases, your estimate is going to be an expression for the independent variable which is going to be called the reversion expression. When dealing with reversion analysis, you are also going to be showing your interest in the characterization of the variation in the dependent variable against the expression which will be described as the probability distribution.

37.
38. One approach that you can take is conditional analysis which is going to take the estimate for the maximum instead of the average of the dependent variables based on the independent variable that is given so that you can decide if the independent variable is necessary but not sufficient for the value that is given to the dependent variable.
39.
40. You are going to use reversion for

forecasting and reversion when it overlaps with machine learning. You will also use it as a way to understand the relationship between the independent and dependent variables. When dealing with a restricted circumstance, you can use reversion to infer the causal relationship between the variables. But, this can end up giving you a false relationship, therefore, you need to be cautious in using reversion.

41.
42. There are some techniques that you can use for reversion like linear reversion or least squares reversion. Your reversion expression is going to be defined in terms of finite numbers which are not going to have a known parameter. Nonparametric reversion is going to be the technique that is used when allowing the reversion expression is going to be used for a set of expressions which may cause infinite dimensional.
43.
44. Your reversion analysis performance is going to be the methods that you practice as a form of data generating processes and how

it ties into the reversion approach that you use. Being that the true form of data generating is not always going to be known since reversion analysis will then depend on the extent of the assumptions that you are making.

45.
46. Your assumptions need to be testable to see if there is a sufficient amount of data being provided.

47. Chapter Four: Python and Machine Learning

48.

49. Python is a coding program that is going to be able to be used for a lot of coding that you are going to want to do in order to write out your own programs. Being that Python is going to be giving you outcomes based on the inputs that you give it means that it is going to use machine learning.

50.

51. Some of what Python does is going to be unsupervised. However, there are going to be parts of it that are going to be supervised due to the fact that you are going to be looking for a specific outcome.

52.

53. In the event that you plan to use Python to leverage the machine learning that you are doing, there are some basic things that you are going to need to know just in case you do not know them. Thankfully, Python is versatile enough that you are going to be able to take the scientific computing that

you are going to be doing with the program and convert it over to machine learning.

54.

55. If you have not already, you are going to need to install Python onto your PC. You are also going to need a package that is going to work with machine learning. It is recommended that you install anaconda due to the fact that it is an industrial strength implementation that is going to be able to be used on any operating system and is going to contain every package that is required when working with machine learning.

56.

57. What you consider a data scientist is going to depend on what you are using machine learning for due to the fact that many data scientists are going to use machine learning algorithms to some level. Because of this, you are going to need to understand the various kernel methods so that you can gain insight from the support vector machine models that they are going to be using.

58.

59. When dealing with data science, you are

going to need to load your data into the program. The discipline that you are going to be using is going to work with data that is observed and collected by you. You are going to need to load the numbers data set in from the Python library, this is going to be called scikit-learn.

60.

61. In order to load in your data, you are going to bring your module into Python with dataset from the sklearn library. From there you are going to have the ability to use the load numbers () expression from the data set that you bring into Python.

62.

63. Syntax

64.

65. From sklearn bring in

66.

67. Numbers = datasets. load numbers ()

68.

69. Produce (____)

70.

71. You should notice that the dataset module is going to hold other methods that are going

to be loaded in order to fetch the most popular reference to the data set that you are using. This means that you can also count on the module to work in the event that you need an artificial data generator.

72.

73. Note: if you download data then it is already going to be separated between test sets and training sets. You are going to be able to tell the difference because the extensions which will be. tar and. tes. both of these files are going to need to be loaded in order to elaborate your project.

74.

75. Whenever you first are working with a data set, you need to look at the data explanation in order to see what you are going to be learning from that data set. In using scikit-learn is not going to make the information readily available to you, however, if you download the data from a different source, you are going to typically find this explanation so that you have enough information to learn more about your data.

76.

77. Keep in mind that these insights are not going to be deep enough for what you are going to be using the data for. You are also going to want to perform an exploratory data analysis on your data set so that you can see how difficult it is going to be to use that data set.

78.

79. If you have not already checked your explanation or you want to double check it, you are going to want to pay special attention to the basic information.

80.

81. The numbers data is going to be produced out once it has been loaded thanks to scikit-learn datasets. Chances are you are going to know a lot of the information that you are going to be looking at like your target values. You are also going to have the ability to access the numbers data by using the attribute data module. This is the same way that you are going to be able to access the target values with the target attribute. The explanation is going to be accessed through the descry attribute.

82.

83. Should you want to look at which essential s are available for your data, you are going to use the numbers. essential () expression.

84.

85. Example

86.

87. #getting the essential s for your digit data

88.

89. Produce (numbers. ___)

90.

91. #producing out the data you are using

92.

93. Produce (numbers. ___)

94.

95. #accessing your target values

96.

97. Produce (numbers. ___)

98.

99. #getting your explanation for your data set

100.

101. Produce (numbers. descr)

102.

103. Should you use the read_csv () expression to bring in your data, you are going to be

looking at a data frame that will contain only your data, and there is not going to be any explanation for the data that you are working with. In this case, you are going to have the option of resorting to the head () or tail () expression to inspect the data. When you are using these methods, you need to ensure you are reading the explanation for your data!

104.

105. Now the question becomes how are you going to access the arrays for your data? The answer is that you will use the attributes that are associated with the array. You need to keep in mind that the attributes are going to become available whenever you use the numbers. essential s () expression. For example, if you use the data attribute to isolate your data then you are going to use the target expression to locate the target values as well as the descr for the explanation.

106.

107.   But what happens now?

108.

109. The first thing is that you need to figure out the number of dimensions that is created by the number of items that are in your array. Your arrays shape is going to be a tuple that is going to tell you exactly how big each dimension is going to be.
110.
111. Example
112.
113. Y = pi. Zeros ((4, 2, 5)) which means that your array is going to be shaped to the (4, 2, 5) points.
114.
115. To see the shape of the arrays you are going to use the data, target, and descr expressions.
116.
117. First, you are going to use the data expression to isolate the numpy array from your digit data before you use the attribute shape so that you can discover what shape the array is going to make. You can also use target and descr to do the same thing. Another attribute that you can use is images which are going to show you the data in an

image rather than just in numbers.

118.
119.   Example
120.
121.   #separate your numbers data
122.
123.   numbers_data = numbers. data
124.
125.   #look at the shape of your array
126.
127.   Produce (shape for the numbers data)
128.
129.   #isolate the target values
130.
131.   Numbers_ target = numbers. ___
132.
133.   #look at the shape again
134.
135.   Produce (target expression)
136.
137.   #produce the number of unique labels that you have
138.
139.   Number_ numbers = Len (np. Unique (numbers. Target))

140.

141.   #isolate your image

142.

143.   Numbers_ images = numbers. Images

144.

145.   #look at the shape once more

146.

147.   Produce (image shape)

148.

149. The last thing that you see in the example is the image data which is going to contain the dimensions of your shape. You are going to be able to visually check the image and the data expressions by relating to the reshaping of your image so that it is no longer 3D but 2D. You will do this by using numbers. images. reshape (instances and pixels). You can also use a long bit of script if you want to be completely sure about the reshaping of the image.

150.

151.   Produce (np. All (numbers. Images. Reshape ((instances and pixels)) == numbers. Data))

152.

153. When working with the numpy method, you will use the all () method so that you can test the elements in the array that are along the axis to see if they evaluate as true. If they come back as true, then the image that you reshaped is going to be equal to your numbers. Data expression.

154.

155. If you feel confident with what you know how to do, you can move up to the next level by visualizing the images that you are working with. Python has a data visualization library that is known as matplotlib for this very purpose.

156.

157.   Syntax

158.

159. Bring in matlotlib pyplot as plt

160.

161.   Fig = plt. Figure (fig size = 6, 6))

162.   Fig. subplots_ adjust (left = 0, right= 1, bottom = 0 top = 1 hspace = 0.05, wspace = 0.05

163.

164.   For I in range (64):

165.

166.   Ax = fig. add_ subplot (8, 8, I + 1, xticks = [], yticks = [])

167.

168.   Ax. imshow (numbers. Images [I] cmap = plt.cm. binary, interpolation = 'nearest')

169.

170.   Ax. Text (0, 7, str (numbers. target [i]))

171.

172.   Plt. Show ()

173.

174.   While the script you just saw is going to be a lot to put into your program and may even seem overwhelming, you can break the script down into chunks so that it is easier to understand.

175.

1. The matplotlib. pyplot must be brought in
2. Then you are going to set up your figure with the size so that you can create your subplots as to where your image is going to appear
3. The subplots are going to set your parameters so that you can adjust how your image is laid out.

4. Once you have done that, you are going to fill up your figure
5. You will need to initialize the subplots by adding each to the appropriate position on the grid.
6. After you have filled your figure, you will then initialize the subplots
7. Each dot that you add is going to display your image on the grid like a color map. The interpolation method is going to mean that the data you are putting on the grid is interpolated so that it is not smooth.
8. The last bit is going to be the text that is added to your subplots.
9. You cannot forget to plot your points with the plt. show () expression

10.

11. Chapter Five: Neural Networks and Deep Learning

12.

13. Neural networks are going to be programming paradigms that are biologically inspired to enable a PC to learn from data that is observed.

14.

15. Deep learning is a set of techniques that you are going to use for neural networks.

16.

17. Both neural networks and deep learning is going to give you the best solution to any problem that you may come up with when you are working with image, speech and natural language recognition and processing.

18.

19. The human visual system is complex and one of the most interesting things that you can study because you are never going to fully understand how it works with the other parts of your body.

20.

21. Take handwriting, for instance, many people are going to be able to look at something that is written and be able to tell you what is written without any problem, but the little effort that it takes to recognize what is written is actually deceptive. If you look at the different hemispheres of your brain, you are going to realize that your visual cortex has several millions of neurons that are going to be connected. However, your vision is not going to be connected to your visual cortext but instead a series of cortices that involve your vision, therefore, making it to where you can process even the most complex of images.
22.
23. Inside of your head is essentially a superPC that has been finetuned by evolution. The ability to recognize handwriting is not always easy, but your brain has adapted to where you are going to be able to do it unconsciously. It is not very often that we take the time to think of how complex our visual system truly is.
24.

25. Just like it is difficult to recognize visual patterns, a PC is not going to have these issues. But, it is going to be different than how we do it ourselves. Our brains recognize shapes and how things are written out, but how to do you tell a PC this? You are going to have to make out rules, and those rules are going to end up getting lost int he exceptions and caveats that you are going to have to create.
26.
27. The neural network approach is going to look at the problem in a different way though. It is going to take a large number of numbers that are handwritten and be trained to recognize the various shapes so that it is able to do what our brain can do. Essentially, the neural network is going to use the examples that are inside of the data you input to infer to rules that are set in place as their way to recognize handwritten numbers. The more you add to the number of examples that train the program, the network is going to be able to learn more handwriting options in order to improve its

accuracy.

28.

29. Neural networks are going to work with an artificial neuron that is known as a perceptron which was developed in the 60s by Frank Rosenblatt. But, when we look at it today, it is going to be used like other models of artificial neurons. Your main neuron is going to be known as the sigmoid neuron; but, to understand the sigmoid neuron you have to understand the perceptrons.

30.

31. Perceptrons are going to take several binary inputs and give you a single binary outcome. Rosenblatt came up with a single rule that will be used when dealing with the outcome of perceptrons. This is where weights came in as a way to express real numbers and their importance to the inputs and outcomes. The outcome for the neuron is going to either be zero or one and determine the weight of the sum and if it is less than or greater than the threshold value.

32.

33. Your threshold value is going to be a real number that is going to be used in the parameters for the neuron. Think of the perceptron as a device that is going to make its decisions by weighing the evidence.
34.
35. For example, if you want to go on a family outing, there are several things that you are going to have to look at to determine if you are going to be able to go on the outing as planned.
36.

1. Is the car big enough for everyone that wants to go?
2. Is the weather going to be good?
3. What do you need to pack for the amount of time that you are going to be out?
4.
5. Each factor is going to be able to be represented by a binary variable. By looking at the weights and the threshold for your problem, you are going to be able to create different models for the decision making process. Your perceptron will decide if you are going to be able to go on your outing or

not. When you drop the threshold, you are going to most likely be able to go on your outing with your family.

6.
7. Keep in mind that your perceptron is not going to be a complete model of the decision-making process that a human can do. However, your preceptron is going to be able to weigh different evidence in order to make the decisions that you need to be made, which should seem more plausible for a complex network of perceptrons that are going to make small decisions that you may not notice are being made.

8.
9. While a learning algorithm sounds like the way to go, how are you going to create an algorithm for a neural network? Think about if you have a network for your perceptrons that you can use in order to solve problems. The inputs to the network are going to be like the raw pixel data that is scanned into the program so that the network has the ability to learn weights and biases in order for the outcome to be classified correctly. If

you make any changes to the weight in the network, your outcome is going to correspond with the change that you made.

10.

11. However, the reality of perceptrons is that when a change is made to the weigh
12. ts, then there is the possibility that the perceptron is going to flip completely due to that change. This change is going to cause the behavior of your entire network to change completely into a more complex behavior. So, while one of your numbers is going to be classified correctly, your network is going to be behaving in a way that is going to be hard to control.

13.

14. Your network's new behavior is going to make it difficult to see how your weights and bases need to be modified so that your network is closer to the behavior that you are wanting. Therefore, there must be a clever way for getting around this issue that may not be obvious instantly.

15.

16. You can overcome the problem just by

bringing in a new neuron known as the sigmoid neuron. These neurons are going to be like perceptrons, but they are going to be modified so that when you make small changes, they are only going to give you a small change in your outcome rather than chancing that your outcome changes completely. This is vitally important and the sigmoid neuron is going to be enabled to learn the behavior of the network.

17.
18. Your sigmoid neuron is going to have inputs that are similar to your perceptron however it is going to be able to take any value that falls between zero and one which means that you can use the decimal points that fall between these two numbers as a valid input for your sigmoid neuron. Just like a perceptron, your sigmoid is going to have a weight for every input as well as a bias that covers everything in that neuron. However, your outcome is not going to be zero or one, it is going to be known as a sigmoid expression, and it is going to be defined by this equation.

19.

20. $\sigma(z) \equiv 1/1+e^{-z}$

21.

22. Another way to look at it is to put the outcomes of your sigmoid neuron with your inputs.

23.

24. $1/1+\exp(-\sum_j w_j x_j - b)$

25.

26. When you first look at your sigmoid neuron, they are going to look very different than your perceptrons. However, the algebraic expression for the sigmoid expression is going to seem opaque and like you are never going to be able to master it. However, you are going to be able to because there are a lot of similarities between your perceptrons and your sigmoid neurons.

27.

28. In an effort to understand the similarities you need to look at a perceptron model like $z \equiv w \cdot x + b$ where you have a large positive number. Which then means $e-z \approx 0 e-z \approx 0$ and $\sigma(z) \approx 1$ are equal. Ultimately, your sigmoid neuron is going to be a large positive number just like it would be for the perceptron.

29.

30. Now, think of it as if you were working with negative numbers, then your sigmoid's behavior will be the same as the perceptron. The only time you are going to see a deviation from your perceptron model is of modest size.

31. But, what is your mathematical form of σ? The truth of the matter is that the exact form of this variable is not brought inant because we are going to want to focus on the shape of our expression.

32.

33. Should this function be a step expression, then your sigmoid neuron is going to end up being a perceptron due to the fact that the outcome would be either zero or one depending on if your equation gives you a positive or negative outcome.

34.

35. When you use the function for σ, then you are going to get a perceptron that is smooth.

While how smooth your expression is, is bring inant, it is not something you need to spend a lot of time focusing on. The smoothness is simply going to modify the weights and bias which is then going to change the outcome for your sigmoid neuron.

36.

37. Thanks to calculus your outcome is going to be predicted by this equation.

38.

39. $\Delta \text{outcome} \approx \sum_j \partial \text{outcome} / \partial w_j \Delta w_j + \partial \text{outcome} / \partial b \, \Delta b,$

40.

41. Your sum that is found over all of your weights and your outcome is going to show a partial derivative for your outcome with the respect that is needed for your weights. You should not get too worried if you find that you are not comfortable working with partial derivatives. Your expression above is going to look complex due to all of the partial derivatives that are in it, but you are actually going to see that it is fairly simple by looking at your outcome as a linear expression. The linearity is going to be easy to pick out smaller changes that are done to the weights and bases to get out the change that you want in your outcome. Therefore, your sigmoid neuron is going to have the same behavior as the perceptron which is going to make it to where it is easier for you to figure out how to change your weights and biases to change the outcome.

42.

43. If the shape is what matters most, then it is not going to be an exact form which is going to be the reason for the use of the o in the equation. When you are looking at the changes that cause you to use a different activation expression, then the value for that partial derivative is going to change the equation. So, when you compute those derivatives later, your function is going to take the algebra and simplify it so that the exponentials have properties that you can work with when differentiated.

44.

45. As you interpret your outcome that comes from the sigmoid neuron you are going to

see that one of the biggest differences is going to be the perceptrons and the neurons where the neurons do not outcome zero or one. They can have any outcome as long as the outcome is a real number and it falls between zero and one. This is going to be useful when you want your outcome to represent the average intensity for the pixels that are in an image. However, sometimes this is going to be a problem.

46.

47. Take for instance you want your outcome to say that your image is nine or is not nine. It is going to be easier to do this in the event that your outcome is zero or one for your perceptron. But, in practice, you are going to have to set up a convention to deal with this so that you can interpret the outcome for at least half of the image which is going to indicate the number you want it to actually be. This means that any outcome that is less than half means that the outcome is not going to be what you want it to be.

48. Chapter Six: Installing Free Datasets for Machine Learning

49.

50. The datasets that you use for machine learning are going to need to be the datasets that have been cited in the peer review academic journals.

51.

52. Datasets are just another part of machine learning that you need to know. You will see major advancements in the field of machine learning just by learning the various pieces of PC hardware as well as the algorithms that are used along with the availability that is offered from the high-quality training datasets.

53.

54. These datasets are going to be supervised as well as semi supervised when dealing with algorithms due to the difficulty and the expansiveness that comes from having to produce the algorithms because of how much time is needed for the data to be labeled. However, if they do not need to be

labeled they can be unsupervised, but this is also going to be costly for a company to produce.

55.

56. The datasets that you can use are for image data which would be things such as recognizing faces or actions, as well as recognizing handwriting and characters that are placed on a piece of paper.

57.

58. Text data is going to be things such as messages that you send to other people, reviews that you leave online, Twitter and Facebook posts that you make, essentially any text that you put into your program.

59.

60. The sound data will be sounds and such as speech and music that can be inserted.

61.

62. Physical data is going to be data collected from astronomy, earth science, and other systems that can physically be measured in some way or another.

63.

64. Signal data is the data that can track electricity or other motions such as how traffic moves through an intersection.

65.

66. Your multivariate data is going to be the data that tracks weather, census, internet traffic, and even your finances.

67. Lastly, the biological datasets are going to measure things such as drug discovery, plant growth, animal growth, and even human growth. Essentially anything that is living can be measured with biological data.

68.
69.
70.
71.
72.

73. PART 2

74.

75.

76. Chapter One: Data Analytic Basics

77.

78. The process of analyzing statistics is going to refer to when you take statistics and break it up into several different components

that then will be examined in individual sets. You are going to gather raw statistics and turn it into a set of useful information that is then going to be used by you or someone else in making decisions for the company or themselves. The statistics that you use are mostly going to be collected to answer questions that will then be used to test a hypothesis or disprove a theory.

79.
80. There are going to be several distinct phases that you are going to go through just to be able to work with the statistics that you have collected to get the statistics analyzed. Do not be surprised if one of the phases that we are about to discuss requires you to have to do some extra work from the previous step so that you get the appropriate statistics inquiry.

81.
82. **Statistics requirements**
83.
84. The statistics that must be placed into the inquiry program are going to depend on the requirements that are established by the

person who is making decisions or the customer who is going to be receiving the product that is created thanks to the statistics that has been analyzed. Most of the statistics that are being analyzed will be collected through an innovative process such as how many people are living in that area. These variables are then broken down into individuals who fit into specific age groups, income status so on and so forth for what statistics needs to be obtained. The statistics that are collected are going to be numerical or categorical depending on what requirements are placed on the gathering of the statistics.

85.

86. The gathering of statistics

87.

88. Whenever you are collecting the statistics that will be used for inquiry, you need to ensure that you are following all the requirements that are set in place for the study that you are working on. You can use environmental sensors such as traffic cameras to collect statistics, or you can do it in a face to face situation, or by using an online source.

89.

90. Processing statistics

91.

92. Once the statistics have been collected, it must go through a process where it is organized so that it can be analyzed. A clear majority of the time you are going to be creating some sort of visual aid so that the statistics are easy to see. For example, you are going to can take the answers that you got from a smoking survey and use Excel to place each response you go to the questions that you asked into the spreadsheet so that the person who is making the decisions can see each response individually rather than having to look at a jumble of statistics that may not make much sense.

93.

94. Statistics cleaning

95.

96. After the statistics have been prepared and organized, you may realize that there are

some errors, duplications, or incomplete statistics entries in what was collected. This is where you are going to go through and clean up the statistics so that your results are not skewed due to statistics that cannot be used. For example, when there are words that have been mistyped, then you are going to have to stop and take the time to figure out what the word is before you can continue in your process of analyzing the statistics; however, when you clean the statistics up before analyzing it, you will not need to take this extra time to figure out what the word was supposed to be.

97.
98. **Exploring Statistics Inquiry**
99.
100. At this point in time, the information that has been collected is going to go through the inquiry process. The person that is doing the analyzing will have the ability to apply various techniques that are going to be known as exploring statistics inquiry so that they can attempt to understand what patterns are inside of that statistics set. The

process of exploration is going to end up causing more statistics to come into play which will then either mean that statistics must be cleaned up once again or additional statistics needs to be collected for the result to be complete.

101.

102. Descriptive statistics is going to be when the average of the statistics is used in seeking to understand the statistics that are being analyzed.

103.

104. Statistics visualization is going to be done much like when you processed the statistics. You are wanting to provide the person making the inquiry with an easier route to identify patterns that may be occurring in the statistics.

105.

106.

107. **Layout and algorithms**

108.

109. The algorithm layout that is used is going to be identifying any correlation between the

statistics points and the variables that are associated with them.

110.

111. Inferential statistics refers to the techniques that are being used to measure any relationships that lie between a set of variables.

112.

113. Regression inquiry is going to use a layout to show where the independent variable was changed as well as illustrate how this change affected the dependent variable.

114.

115.

116. When using algorithms, you are going to be using the x and y variables just like you would with any other mathematical equation.

117.

118. Statistics Product

119.

120. The result that is produced from your inquiry will be placed on a computer application which will then give you an

outcome that you may not have been able to reach without that software.

121. The product from your statistics may be based upon an algorithm that you had to make in the last step. An example of statistics product is when a customer bought something and based on that purchasing history; other purchases are recommended for them that they may find themselves enjoying.

122.

123. Communication

124.

125. After you have completed all the other steps, you are now ready to share the statistics that you have analyzed. The result is to acquire feedback from your customer that is going to assist your company in the running more efficiently in ensuring that you are getting the product out that your clients are wanting.

126.

127. Sometimes you are going to have to use statistics visualization to share the statistics that you have collected and analyzed with others so that they can see what it is that you see in the statistics.

128.

129. Chapter Two: Challenges for Data Analytics

130.

131. It does not matter what type of statistics you are working with; you are going to run into some problems that are ultimately going to slow you down. Sometimes the type of statistics that you are analyzing is going to cause the problem, while other times it is going to be how the statistics were collected, or the responses that were received.

132.

133. Whether you are working with big statistics or standard statistics, the statistics are going to affect your enterprise in at least three significant ways.

134.

1. Automate enterprise processes: with automated enterprise processes, you are going to be looking at stock trading that may have been derailed to identify any patterns that may be there which may have led to a trade that was poorly executed, thus automating the process to cause the pattern to happen once more.
2. Discover insights that are hidden: you may have had your customers complete a survey and the statistics that you get from the study are going to be used to see why there are so many cancellations at your hotel. In this statistic, you may be able to see a pattern or some other reason that you were not able to distinguish before therefore allowing you to improve the retention rate of your customers.
3. Improve decisions through the enrichment of information that is given to the decision makers: looking at things such as social media pages, you are going to have the

ability to gain more insight to your client which will then aid you in providing a better service or product for them.

4.
5. While these impacts can be good or bad for your company, the tests that you face are going to be tied to each of them.
6.
7.
8. These tests must be addressed promptly to make sure that you are having success in your enterprise.
9.
   1. Solution cost: most of the statistics that you are working with is going to be accompanied by a cost. So, to make sure you have had a positive ROI, you are going to need to reduce the cost of any solutions that need to be used to figure out the value that you are looking for. If you do not need to spend money, then you shouldn't. While that is a no brainer, not everyone is going to realize that

the method they choose is going to be so expensive, therefore, you should look at all the costs that will come with every method you are thinking of using, and see where you can cut some of your expenses but still get to the outcome that you are wanting.

2.

3. Statistics integration: sometimes you are going to be working with statistics that is not similar, but it still must be combined so that you can see all of it. What you are going to have to do is find a solution that is going to allow for you to combine all the statistics quickly and at a reasonable cost. On top of that, you are going to be faced with the test of figuring out how you are going to control the statistics quality so that you can understand your statistics.

4.

5. Skills availability: there are always new tools that are coming out that you are going to be able to use so that you can analyze statistics

in a unique way. However, there is a shortage of individuals that are capable of the skills that are needed to bring all the statistics together so that it can be analyzed and published.
6.
7. With this shortage, you are going to be forced to create a solution that not only allows you to use the new tools, but you are going to want to keep it inside of your budget.
8.
9. Statistics volume: most of the time you are going to be working with a large volume of statistics and the issue that you are going to run into is being able to process that volume at an acceptable speed so that you can look at the information that is available to you and get it to those that are making the decisions.
10.
11. Depending on the software that you are using will depend on how fast the statistics

can be processed, and this is where having people that have the skillset needed to work with this software comes into play. Having someone who can manipulate the program so that it does not slow down due to the volume of statistics.

12.

13. Looking at the tests that you are going to be presented with when it comes to working with statistics analytics, you are going to realize that these are tests that every company must work against to be successful.

14.

15.

16. You may discover that you are face to face with a few tests that were not mentioned here, the only thing that you are going to be able to do to come up with a solution to get past the tests is to take it one step at a time and do not allow yourself to get overwhelmed or else you are not going to find the appropriate solution to the tests that you are facing with your statistics inquiry.

17.

18.

19. Chapter Three: Terms You Need to Know for Data Analysis

20.

21. Statistics is constantly growing, there are many statistics pieces that you are going to be able to analyze and if you know the keywords that are going to describe the processes that you are using, then it is going to be easier for you to be able to explain what it is that you are doing to someone else who knows about statistics analytics. Not to mention, you are going to be able to describe what it is that must be done without getting it confused with something else.

22.

1. Predictive modeling: whenever you predict an outcome based on the records and variables that are at your disposal whenever the target has been known. The learning layout that you use is going to either be statistical or machine, and they will be

trained to take the statistics that are known and place it where it needs to go so that the outcome becomes unknown to you. This includes the classification and the prediction of the outcome as well.

2.
3. Predictive Analytics: this is the same process that you used for predictive modeling except that you are going to be less specific and technical about the outcome. Most of the time you are just describing the field in general.
4.
5. Supervised learning: this is another name that can be used for predictive modeling.
6.
7. Unsupervised learning: the mining method that you use for statistics will not include your prediction of what the end will be because of the training layout that you have for the statistics in which the outcome you have will be known. An unsupervised method

is going to include outlier detection, cluster inquiry, association rules, dimension reduction and several other methods to figure out your outcome.

8.
9. Enterprise intelligence: this term is older and is going to be used when talking about how you will extract any information that is useful from the statistics without using any sort of learning model.
10.
11. Statistics mining: depending on the context of this word, it can hold several different meanings. When it comes to using it in an analyst, this word typically means that the machine and statistical learning machine methods are collected and put into statisticsbases that are then used for predictive modeling, so on and so forth.
12.

13. Text mining: this is the same thing as statistics mining except that it is going to be done with text.
14.
15. Text Analytics: this is a broad term that is going to be done before you can do any text mining or mining in general. There are specialized applications that are going to be used for things such as sentiment inquiry. When you prepare the text for inquiry, then you are going to be using automated parsing and some sort of interpretation before it is then quantified.
16.
17. Statistics science, statistics analytics, analytics: statistics science is most often used when defining a profession in which the practitioners are knowledgeable in an area of statistics inquiry. Statistics analytics, as well as the analytics, is going to be a general term that is used when trying to describe the gathering and inquiry of statistics.
18.

19. Statistics: this term is going to cover all the conditions that we talked about above. Statistics also refers to a profession that is well established and came about in the 1800s. many statisticians are going to work with problems that come from big statistics fields, and they are traditionally going to be focused on research studies such as drug trials.
20.
21. Big statistics: the massive amounts of statistics that an organization collects. This statistic is usually unstructured but can also be structured such as a transaction statisticsbases.
22.
23. Machine learning: a computer is going to learn from the statistics that are going to then output layout that the statistics must follow. Predictive modeling is going to be included in the machine learning. However, a characteristic of the techniques used for

machine learning is going to give you a model that is flexible and will ultimately adapt to the statistics that is being used. The statistical modeling methods will have a highly structured form. The unsupervised learning methods are going to be associated with rules and clusters, but they are also part of machine learning.

24.

25. Network analytics: when you are attempting to describe the visualization of the various connections that occur between objects.

26.

27. Social network analytics: this will be the inquiry of the relationships that occur between humans. statisticsbases usually happens on websites such as Facebook.

28.

29. Web analytics: the statistical or machine learning methods that occur on the internet.

30.

31. Uplift or persuasion modeling: there will be a combination of the treatment comparisons along with predictive modeling which is going to be determined by how the subject responds to the treatments. There are some steps you will follow for a typical uplift model.
   a. Perform a test with two subjects where the second subjects are the control.
   b. All the statistics from both groups will need to be combined.
   c. Separate the statistics into different segments to where there is roughly the same number from each test group. You may want to use a tree method for this.
   d. You need to have your segments drawn in such a way that each of your segments show the difference between the response and the control groups.
   e. Look at each section as a unit that is a model that will then predict If the subject is going to react positively to the treatment or not.
   f.

g. Your test is going to come when you are trying to recognize that the model does not have the ability to operate on the individual cases and if the subject is from group a or from group b, however, it cannot be from both. Therefore, the uplift is going to be the treatment and how the subjects reacted compared to the control group. Hence why you are going to need segments to see the differences.

h.
i. Chapter Four: Benefits of Data Analysis
j.
k. When you can enhance your product or the value of the service that you are offering to your client. Then your client is going to be satisfied which is then going to bring more enterprise to your company because you are meeting or even succeeding your client's expectations.
l. The target market for all the industries around the world is dynamic which causes their needs to frequently change so that they can try and get ahead of their competition. To pull ahead of their competition, many companies come up with new innovations that they hope will meet the expectations that their customers have of them.
m.
n.
o. Before statistics analytics came to what it is that we know it as today, those that were in the enterprise industry had to work with the layout of statistics that had been analyzed but was full of holes and errors which ended

up putting a hindrance on their production and any plans that they had in the works. Since there was not any constructive way to be able to organize the statistics that was extracted from the inquiry that happened earlier. The enterprises that started with statistics inquiry, in the beginning, had to work harder to try and get information from their customers to provide a service that was appreciated.

p.

q. When statistics are collected for statistical inquiry, what you are going to be doing is using it for decision making in pursuing your companies goal. Any mistake that is made or error that is overlooked can cause the company a delay in its decisions that are meant to push the company towards the goals that they want to achieve. If you are not careful, then your enterprise could even come to a complete halt because of the mistakes that have been overlooked.

r.

s. However, how will statistics analytics benefit your company?

t.
1. The analytics is going to assist you in measuring how much of your mission statement has been achieved.
2.
3. Any good enterprise is going to have a mission statement that is going to tell their customers what their goals are and what their marketing plan is so that they can look at see how much progress their company has made. In the end, you are going to have to ensure that your mission statement has goals that are tangible and that are going to end up bringing in a profit for your company.
4.
5. These values are going to be able to be analyzed which is ultimately going to make it to where you can see if you are still on the road to making sure that your company is keeping to the goals that you have set forth, or if you should reevaluate your company's goals and rewrite your mission statement.
6.
7. Whenever your employees have a clear view of what they are expected to do, then they

are going to be more informed which is going to cause them to be more productive cause they know what you are looking at when it comes to evaluation time.

8.

9. Smart decision making will be encouraged.

10.

11. Having important statistics accessible to those that need to have permission to view it will allow the company to have the power to make decisions that are accurate and going to assist in pushing the enterprise past their competition. With this useful statistic, the company is going to be able to assess it and make their decisions faster and more efficiently than what they could before.

12.

13. When a company takes analytics and uses them to their full potential, they are going to be able to take these statistics to their employees and get a fresh perspective on what they got from their inquiry. This opens the option for employees to put their input in that will enable the enterprise to take the steps necessary to reach their objective

while making decisions that are more informed rather than relying on a single person to analyze the statistics which can lead to statistics being misread and decisions to be made that are not the smartest decisions for the company's success.

14.

15. A clear insight into the use of statistics visualization

16.

17. Just like technology, analytics has evolved in how statistics are presented to the inquiry team. The charts and graphs that are used to show the statistics in a way that allows for the inquiry team to make the decisions that they need to make because they are going to be more informed of the patterns that are in the statistics that has been collected.

18.

19. Not only that, but your statistics are going to be presented in a way that is visually appealing for your decision team to look at, but it is going to be organized in a way that is not going to cause them to have to sit and

scratch their heads as they attempt to figure out what it is that they are looking at.

20.

21. Your analytics will keep you up to date

22.

23. It is the typical mindset of consumers to change what it is that they want which causes the market to change since the customer is typically looking for the best offer that is out there on the market at that time. With the use of analytics, you are going to have the insight that is going to show you what your customer is most likely going to be swayed by therefore you are going to be able to keep your customers even though they are constantly changing their minds.

24.

25. With all the shifts in the market happening rapidly, it is not too hard to see why the larger companies typically buy up promising startups so that they can try and keep profits coming in. To keep your enterprise protected, you are going to use analytics so that you can be innovative and change your company to meet the needs and wants of

your customers.

26.

27. Analytics offer your company efficiency

28.

29. Thanks to statistics inquiry, enterprises can be more efficient in their production because they are not going into the market blind. Collecting copious amounts of statistics and presenting it in a way that is visually appealing allows for companies to make decisions that are going to assist them in reaching the goals that they want to reach.

30.

31. Analytics also helps to encourage a company's culture of efficiency as well as promoting teamwork by allowing the employees to voice their insights when it comes to the decision-making process. Another option is that analytics is going to give a company the best choice in where they should try and push their enterprise in reaching new goals rather than staying stagnant and eventually fading out.

32.

33. Chapter Five: The Risks Involved with Data Analysis

34.

35. Projects that consist of a lot of statistics are always going to come with risks. There are many risks that a project can be exposed to are things like under budgeting, lack of individuals that know what they are doing, and bad management. However, your project will contain its own risks on top of the risks that were mentioned above.

36.

37. Because of the improvements in technology, there are always going to be new skill sets that are going to have to be acquired to work with these new advances. If you are not careful, then you are not only opening yourself up to failure, but you are also putting yourself at risk for legal issues as well.

38.

39. Many enterprise people are going to be used to dealing with risks. However, they are going to assess those risks and decide if

they are worth taking or not. Not only that, but others are going to come up with some safeguards that are going to make it to where they are able to protect themselves so that they are not risking their enterprise or their statistics.

40.

41. To comprehend what you need to protect yourself from, you need to know what risks are out there when it comes to statistics analytics so that you can find a way to protect yourself, your statistics, and your company.

42.

1. Statistics security

2.

3. Security is, of course, the first thing that is going to come to the minds of any enterprise person that is going to be working with statistics. They do not want an opposing company to get ahold of the statistics that they have and using it to beat them to the newest change that they are trying to accomplish. However, it is not just opposing companies that you need to worry about, you

also need to worry about hackers getting into your system and obtaining personal information about your clients or employees.

4.

5. Whenever information is stolen from a big company, it makes the news, and it is not quickly forgotten since it opens the public's eyes to just how easy it is to get your information, even if they are doing everything they can to protect themselves. One of the companies that you may think of is Target, and how statistics was taken from them, that harmed their customers.

6.

7. The more statistics that your company has, then the bigger target you are creating for criminals. If your company ends up becoming the target of a hacker, then you are putting yourself at risk of losing more money because a judge is going to decide that any settlement will be for those that have been affected by the security breach.

8.

9. Statistics privacy

10.

11. It does not matter what kind of statistics you are working with, it needs to be protected, and its privacy kept to those who need to know the information. The less information that is divulged, the less risk you are opening yourself up to.

12.

13. When you fail to protect your statistics and only allow those who need to have access to it, access to the statistics, then you are going to be opening yourself up to lawsuits and maybe even some prison time if you are not careful. This is also going to depend on the type of statistics that you are currently working with as well as the jurisdiction that you are working in.

14.

15. Costs

16.

17. As we discussed in the previous chapter, there are going to be costs that are associated with collecting statistics, but there are also costs for storing and analyzing said statistics. Let's add in the compliance

costs that you are going to have to pay to try and avoid any issues that may be associated with your statistics.

18.

19. Most of these costs can be worked into your budget because they are not going to come as a surprise, and this is going to come whenever you are in the planning stages of what statistics that you are going to be collecting and what you are doing with that statistic.

20.

21. At the point in time that you can get rid of any statistics that you do not absolutely need, then you are going be able to save yourself some money so that you do not have to go through any unnecessary processes for statistics that you do not need.

22.

23. Bad analytics

24.

25. This is when you misinterpret the statistics that you have gotten ahold of. If you can draw links between the various parts of

statistics, then it is going to be a random coincidence. The statistics that you get from something such as a major sporting event are going to make you want to draw a link to the sports fans versus the amount of product that you could sell since more people were in town for this event. The same would be accurate if there significant any other event that had come to town.

26.

27. While you are not necessarily misinterpreting your statistics, you are not keeping the fact that your sales went up because there were more people in town. The next day or week when those people are no longer in town, you may not see the massive sales that you did that week. Therefore, you may have misread the statistics by assuming that your sales would go up the following week when they would fall or become stagnant.

28.

29. Bad statistics

30.

31. The thing that you must keep an eye out for

is the gathering of statistics that is irrelevant. Bad statistics is usually collected since you did not have enough time to gather the statistics that was needed for the study that you were conducting. This is frequently accompanied by the thought process of "collect everything and sort it out later."

32.

33. With this mindset, you are going to end up spending extra time and money to process the statistics to make sure that you are getting rid of what you do not need.

34.

35. So, to make sure that you are getting the information that you absolutely need, you are going to need to have a series of checks that are going to keep you from having to spend additional time and money.

36.

37. These are some of the most important risks that you are going to have to consider when it comes to dealing with the inquiry of statistics. If you can work through these risks, then you are going to be able to get the right statistics that you are needing for the study that you are currently conducting as well as making sure that you are not spending more money that is in your budget.

38. **An added benefit will be that you are going to be protecting your company from hackers and unhappy customers!**
39.

40. Chapter Six: Types of Statistics Analytics

41.

42. If you have a modest budget, you are going to be able to collect copious amounts of statistics, however just collecting the statistics should not be the end goal for you. The whole reason you are collecting the statistics is to be able to analyze those statistics and find the patterns in the statistics that you collected so that you can improve your enterprise.

43.

44.

45. When you have gotten to the peak the "refinement process" you are going through the analytics process. There are four types of analytics that you are going to be able to choose from when you are in your inquiry process.

46.

1. Optimization: with optimization, you are going to be working with a more complex

model type which is then going to operate off the questions that ask what if. What happens if we do this, or what happens if we do that? A majority of the time, these issues are going to be answered by a marketing agency by coming up with the layout to show what happens when that situation is put into action. This type of analytics is going to be using a different statistics comparison technique instead of using the usual predictive modeling.

2.
3. Enterprise intelligence (BI reporting): BI reporting works more in real time situations. Such as, what has happened in the past thirty days with sales. Did this marking strategy work or should we move on to a different one? You may know this type of analytics as dashboard reporting or even conventional reporting. In the end, with enterprise intelligence, you are going to be working on the real world and what is

happening in the present moment rather than trying to work off what could occur in the future.

4.

5. Predictive analytics: what is going to happen with the statistics that you have collected? With predictive analytics, you are going to be trying to figure out what is going to happen in the future through a carefully statistical model which is going to show you what may occur, but it is not going to be for certain because you are not able to predict what the future is going to do. Predictive inquiry is going to be complicated and is going to allow for statisticians the tools they need to show correlations between the variables in the statistics.

6.

7. Descriptive analytics: by taking the time to profile your customer's thanks to the statistics that you have collected, then you are going to be using descriptive analytics.

With descriptive analytics, you are going to be using methods such as clustering, profiling, and segmentation.

8.
9. Each of these statistics inquiry types is going to be used when it comes to analyzing your statistics. But, it is going to be the statistics type that will ultimately decide which method you are going to use. If one method does not work, then reexamine the statistics and see if there is a method that will work better for you and what you are trying to achieve.
10.

11.

12.

13.

14.

15. Conclusion

Congratulations on making it through *Machine Learning for Beginners*!

It is my hope that you could learn everything that you were wanting to know about machine learning and how it can help you in getting the results that you are wanting when you are working with programs such as Python.

You are not going to be able to always get the outcome that you are wanting since there are going to be mistakes made because you are human. However, you are going to get closer each time that you use machine learning.

Now it is your turn to begin to use what you have learned in this book in your everyday life. You are going to notice that there is a change in how you approach work now that you are armed with this knowledge.

27. About The Author

Hi there it's Jonathan Walker here, I want to share a little bit about myself so that we can get to know each other on a deeper level. I grew up in California, USA, and have lived there for the better part of my life. Being exposed to many different people and opportunities when I was young, it made me want to strive to become an entrepreneur to escape the rat race path that most of my peers had taken. I knew I wanted to be able to travel and experience the world the way it was meant to be seen and I've done just that. I've travelled to most places around the world and I'm enjoying every minute of it for sure. In my free time I love to play tennis and believe it or not, compose songs. I wish you all the best again in your endeavours, and may your dreams, whatever they may be, come true abundantly in the near future.

31.

32.